CHECKERBOARD BIOGRAPHY LIBRARY

U.S. PRESIDENTS

The
United States Presidents

HERBERT HOOVER

ABDO Publishing Company

BreAnn Rumsch

visit us at
www.abdopublishing.com

Published by ABDO Publishing Company, 8000 West 78th Street, Edina, Minnesota 55439. Copyright © 2009 by Abdo Consulting Group, Inc. International copyrights reserved in all countries. No part of this book may be reproduced in any form without written permission from the publisher. The Checkerboard Library™ is a trademark and logo of ABDO Publishing Company.

Printed in the United States of America, North Mankato, Minnesota.
012009 102013

Cover Photo: Getty Images
Interior Photos: AP Images pp. 5, 10, 13, 17, 23; Corbis pp. 19, 21, 27, 29; Getty Images p. 25; iStockphoto p. 32; Library of Congress pp. 14, 15, 18; National Archives p. 16; National Park Service pp. 9, 28

Editor: Megan M. Gunderson
Art Direction & Cover Design: Neil Klinepier
Interior Design: Neil Klinepier

Library of Congress Cataloging-in-Publication Data

Rumsch, BreAnn, 1981-
 Herbert Hoover / BreAnn Rumsch.
   p. cm. -- (The United States presidents)
 Includes index.
 ISBN 978-1-60453-458-0
 1. Hoover, Herbert, 1874-1964--Juvenile literature. 2. Presidents--United States--Biography-- Juvenile literature. I. Title.

 E802.R86 2009
 973.916092--dc22
  [B]
                        2008025595

CONTENTS

HERBERT HOOVER

Herbert Hoover was different from other politicians. Unlike other presidents, he was not a lawyer or even a great speaker. Instead, Hoover was a scientist and a businessman. He became a politician because he wanted to help others.

Hoover's parents died when he was young. So, an uncle raised him in Oregon. Hoover then went to college and became a successful mining **engineer**. During **World War I**, he led relief efforts in Europe. Then, Hoover worked as the U.S. food **administrator** and the **secretary of commerce**.

In 1928, Hoover was elected the thirty-first U.S. president. When he took office, the nation's **economy** seemed strong. But in late 1929, it started to fail.

A long period of hardship fell across America. This time became known as the Great Depression. Many Americans blamed Hoover for their troubles.

Still, Hoover continued to work hard for America. In time, he was recognized for his great contributions to the United States and the world.

Herbert Hoover

TIMELINE

1874 - On August 10, Herbert Clark Hoover was born in West Branch, Iowa.

1885 - Hoover moved to Newberg, Oregon, to live with his uncle.

1895 - Hoover graduated from California's Stanford University, where he studied geology.

1899 - On February 10, Hoover married Lou Henry in California.

1900 - In China, the Hoovers were caught in the Boxer Rebellion.

1908 - Hoover began his own engineering company in London, England.

1914 - World War I began; Hoover headed the Commission for Relief in Belgium.

1917 - President Woodrow Wilson appointed Hoover U.S. food administrator.

1919 - Hoover directed the American Relief Administration.

1921 - Hoover became secretary of commerce under President Warren G. Harding.

1929 - On March 4, Hoover became the thirty-first president of the United States; the stock market crashed in October.

1932 - Hoover established the Reconstruction Finance Corporation; he lost reelection to Franklin D. Roosevelt.

1939 - World War II began; Hoover led the Polish Relief Commission.

1944 - Lou Hoover died on January 7.

1946 - Hoover directed the Famine Emergency Committee.

1947 and 1953 - Hoover served as chairman for the Hoover Commissions.

1964 - On October 20, Herbert Hoover died in New York City, New York.

DID YOU KNOW?

Construction on Hoover Dam began in 1930 along the Colorado River. The dam was finished in 1936. Today, it is the highest concrete arch dam in the United States. The dam was originally named Boulder Dam. In 1947, it was renamed to honor President Herbert Hoover.

Hoover was one of two presidents to give away his presidential salary. He gave his salary to charities. In addition, the Hoovers paid for social events at the White House with their own money.

In 1931, President Hoover signed an act that made "The Star-Spangled Banner" the national anthem.

Hoover loved the outdoors. He especially enjoyed fishing. He even wrote a book about this favorite hobby called *Fishing for Fun*.

YOUNG BERT

Herbert Clark Hoover was born in West Branch, Iowa, on August 10, 1874. Everyone called him Bert. Bert's parents were Jesse and Hulda Hoover. Jesse worked as a blacksmith and sold farm machinery. Bert had a brother, Theodore, and a sister, May.

Bert and his family were **Quakers**. They believed in living a simple life, working hard, and helping others. These values stayed with Bert his whole life.

When Bert was six years old, his father died. Hulda held the family together. She worked as a **seamstress** and a Quaker minister. Sadly, Hulda died when Bert was nine. So relatives took in the Hoover children.

In 1885, Bert moved to Newberg, Oregon. There, he attended a Quaker school called Friends Pacific Academy. Bert lived with his uncle Henry John Minthorn, who was a doctor.

FAST FACTS

BORN - August 10, 1874
WIFE - Lou Henry
            (1874–1944)
CHILDREN - 2
POLITICAL PARTY - Republican
AGE AT INAUGURATION - 54
YEARS SERVED - 1929–1933
VICE PRESIDENT - Charles Curtis
DIED - October 20, 1964, age 90

8

Bert's birthplace in West Branch, Iowa

Three years later, Bert and his uncle moved to Salem, Oregon. In Salem, Minthorn started a **real estate** business. Bert worked there as an office clerk. At night, he took business classes.

Eventually, Bert decided to become an **engineer**. So in 1891, he moved to California. There, he attended a new school called Stanford University.

STUDENT & ENGINEER

At Stanford, Hoover studied geology. He also managed a laundry business, delivered newspapers, and worked for the university. Hoover spent his summers working as an assistant geologist for the U.S. government.

Hoover found time to have fun, too. He managed Stanford's baseball and football teams. He was also elected junior class **treasurer**.

Arthur Diggles
Herbert Hoover
R E McDonnell
James White
SURVEYING SQUAD · STANFORD UNIVERSITY IN 1893

During his last year at Stanford, Hoover met Lou Henry. She was a fellow geology student. Hoover and Lou had much in common. They quickly fell in love.

In 1895, Hoover graduated from Stanford. Then, he took a job in a California gold mine. He pushed a mining car and shoveled ore. Hoover worked long hours and made little money. However, he gained valuable experience.

Hoover took a job with mining **engineer** Louis Janin in 1896. At first, Janin hired Hoover to work only as a typist. But he soon sent Hoover on mining jobs in New Mexico, Colorado, and Arizona.

In 1897, Janin helped Hoover get a job with Bewick, Moreing & Company of London, England. The company sent Hoover to Australia. There, he taught Australians about U.S. mining methods. Hoover also discovered a gold mine. It earned him and the company a great deal of money.

At Stanford, Hoover (lower left) *belonged to a student engineering group. Members of the group practiced surveying, or measuring land.*

WORLD TRAVELER

In 1898, Bewick, Moreing & Company offered Hoover a job in China. Hoover accepted. In a telegram, he proposed marriage to Lou. They were married in California on February 10, 1899. That same day, they boarded a ship to China.

In China, Hoover acted as the chief **engineer** for the Chinese Imperial Bureau of Mines. He helped the Chinese government find many coal fields and minerals.

The Hoovers were caught in the **Boxer Rebellion** in 1900. They lived in a settlement in Tientsin with other foreigners. For almost a month, the settlement was under attack. During that time, Hoover supervised the construction of defenses. He also handed out food and water. Eventually, foreign troops arrived in China to stop the rebellion. The Hoovers had outlasted the danger.

The following year, Hoover became a partner with Bewick, Moreing & Company. On August 4, 1903, the Hoovers welcomed their first son, Herbert Jr. Five weeks later, the family set out on a world journey. Hoover looked for new business for the company. Then on July 17, 1907, the Hoovers had a second son, Allan.

By 1908, the Hoovers had settled in London, England. Hoover was now a wealthy man. He left Bewick, Moreing & Company and formed his own **engineering** company. He started mining projects and helped other companies manage their money.

The Hoover family. Seated are Hoover and his wife, Lou, who holds their granddaughter Peggy Ann. Their son Herbert Jr. (right) stands with his wife, Margaret, and his brother, Allan (left).

PUBLIC SERVICE

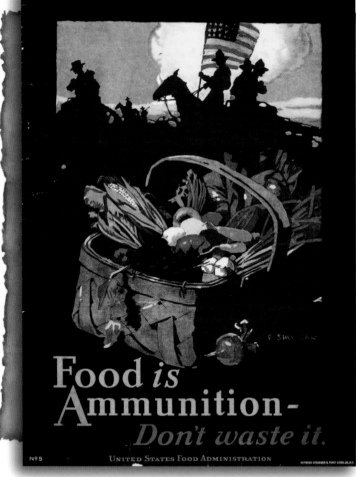

Food *is* Ammunition-
Don't waste it.

N° 5   UNITED STATES FOOD ADMINISTRATION

Posters from the U.S. Food Administration encouraged Americans to observe "Meatless Mondays" and "Wheatless Wednesdays."

Hoover's new business was a success. However, he became bored with simply making money. Hoover wanted to move into public service.

World War I began in Europe in 1914. At the time, Hoover was still living in London. The war trapped thousands of Americans in Europe. Hoover organized a relief committee to help Americans get home safely.

Later that year, a British **blockade** stopped food shipments to Belgium. To help, Hoover headed the Commission for Relief in Belgium. It raised money to feed more than 9 million hungry Belgians.

Hoover also formed other relief efforts during **World War I**. He helped feed and clothe millions of children affected by the war.

In 1917, America entered the war. President Woodrow Wilson called Hoover home and made him

About 14 million U.S. families followed Hoover's food conservation program.

the U.S. food **administrator**. The United States needed to have enough food to send to its troops fighting in Europe. So, Hoover asked Americans to limit the food they ate.

After World War I ended, many people were left homeless and hungry. Hoover directed the American Relief Administration in 1919. It fed 300 million people from 21 countries in Europe and the Middle East.

SECRETARY OF COMMERCE

Hoover's efforts in Europe made him famous. Many Americans thought he would make a good president. He decided to seek the **Republican** nomination for president in 1920.

However, the Republicans chose Warren G. Harding instead. Harding became the next president. Vice President Calvin Coolidge became president when Harding died three years later.

Hoover became the **secretary of commerce** in 1921. He kept the job for almost eight years. Hoover worked under presidents Harding and Coolidge.

The Boulder Canyon Project Act of 1928 authorized the construction of what later became Hoover Dam.

16

As **secretary of commerce**, Hoover accomplished much. He wrote a highway safety code and improved airline safety. Hoover also encouraged industries to standardize their products. This lowered the cost of goods and created new jobs.

In 1921, Hoover planned irrigation and power developments along the Colorado River. His ideas eventually led to the construction of Hoover Dam.

President Coolidge (left) *and Secretary Hoover*

As part of the Better Homes in America campaign, Hoover helped break ground at the construction site for a model home.

In 1923, Secretary Hoover established and became president of the American Child Health Association. This organization improved hospitals and helped sick children in need.

Hoover also served as president of Better Homes in America throughout the 1920s. This organization lowered the cost of new homes. So, more Americans were able to become home owners.

Then in 1927, the Mississippi River flooded. More than 600,000 people were affected by the disaster. Hoover quickly organized a flood relief program. It fed, clothed, and housed many thousands of flood victims.

Hoover's great works continued to make him popular with Americans. In 1928, the **Republican** Party nominated Hoover to run for president. Senator Charles Curtis was nominated for vice president.

The **Democrats** nominated Alfred E. Smith. His **running mate** was Senator Joseph T. Robinson. In the election, voters made Hoover the thirty-first president of the United States.

Curtis (left) *and Hoover campaigned together in 1928.*

PRESIDENT HOOVER

Hoover took office on March 4, 1929. At the time, the United States was experiencing a period of great prosperity. President Hoover wanted every American to share in the nation's wealth. He hoped to see a nation "built of home owners and farm owners."

To help Americans, President Hoover created many new organizations. The Federal Farm Board aided struggling farmers. The Veterans Administration cared for former members of the armed forces. And, the Federal Bureau of Prisons reformed U.S. prisons.

In addition, Hoover pushed Congress to create a Department of Education. He proposed tax cuts for the poor. Hoover also reorganized the Bureau of Indian Affairs. This allowed it to better protect the rights of Native Americans.

The president did not stop there. He proposed a series of dams in Tennessee and California. Hoover established more national parks and monuments. He also enlarged many national forests. These projects created many new jobs.

President Hoover's Cabinet

March 4, 1929–
March 4, 1933

STATE – Henry L. Stimson
TREASURY – Andrew W. Mellon
   Ogden L. Mills (from February 13, 1932)
WAR – James W. Good
   Patrick J. Hurley (from December 9, 1929)
NAVY – Charles Francis Adams
ATTORNEY GENERAL – William D. Mitchell

INTERIOR – Ray Lyman Wilbur
AGRICULTURE – Arthur M. Hyde
COMMERCE – Robert P. Lamont
   Roy D. Chapin (from December 14, 1932)
LABOR – James J. Davis
   William N. Doak (from December 9, 1930)

To aid farmers, Hoover signed the Farm Relief Bill in 1929.

Meanwhile, people had been making money in the **stock market**. However, many had borrowed money to buy stocks they could not afford. Hoover knew this was dangerous for the **economy**.

So, President Hoover asked Congress for tougher banking laws. But Congress ignored Hoover's requests. The banks kept lending money. More and more Americans went into **debt**.

Then in October 1929, disaster struck the U.S. stock market. Stock prices crashed. People who had borrowed money to buy stocks could not repay their loans. Banks began to suffer.

Even worse, many people lost their savings. People had less money to spend, so production slowed and businesses suffered. A **recession** began. President Hoover tried to stop it. He asked business leaders not to fire people or cut their wages. He also asked state leaders to create jobs through **public works**.

But Hoover's plans did not work. The economy continued to slow. By 1931, more than 11 million Americans were out of work. Those who held jobs had their wages cut. Banks began to shut down. The recession turned into the Great Depression. And the economy continued to worsen.

SUPREME
COURT
APPOINTMENTS

CHARLES EVANS HUGHES - 1930
OWEN ROBERTS - 1930
BENJAMIN NATHAN CARDOZO - 1932

22

The stock market crash on October 24, 1929, was the worst financial upset in U.S. history. The day became known as Black Thursday.

THE GREAT DEPRESSION

President Hoover believed America should help itself out of the Great Depression. But he also saw that his plans were failing. So in January 1932, Hoover asked Congress to establish the Reconstruction Finance Corporation (RFC).

The RFC gave government money to large businesses and banks. Hoover hoped the RFC would help these businesses run smoothly again. Then they could give people jobs.

Hoover also asked Congress to approve **public works**. More than 800 public buildings and about 37,000 miles (60,000 km) of highway were built. These projects created many jobs.

Still, families across the nation were homeless. People everywhere waited in long lines for bread. Others marched through Washington, D.C., to demand government relief.

In 1932, Hoover was up for reelection. He ran against New York governor Franklin D. Roosevelt. Roosevelt's **running mate** was **Speaker of the House** John N. Garner. The campaign was

All over the country, homeless people built shack communities. These were called Hoovervilles. Other homeless people slept under newspapers called Hoover blankets.

difficult. Many Americans blamed Hoover for the Great Depression. Roosevelt easily won the election.

Hoover's last days as president were challenging. In February 1933, banks across the country shut down. Hoover tried to turn the **economy** around. However, he did not have time to fix the nation's problems. The Great Depression would not end until 1942.

AFTER THE WHITE HOUSE

After leaving the White House in March 1933, the Hoovers retired to two homes. One was in Palo Alto, California. The other was an apartment in the Waldorf-Astoria Hotel in New York City, New York.

Hoover stayed busy. In 1936, he served as chairman of the Boys Club of America. With Hoover's help, 500 new clubs were started. They gave homeless boys a safe place to go.

In 1939, **World War II** began when Germany attacked Poland. Hoover led the Polish Relief Commission. The organization provided food for thousands of Polish children during the war.

Then on January 7, 1944, Lou Hoover suffered a heart attack and died. Hoover missed his wife very much.

World War II ended in 1945. It had destroyed cities and caused food shortages across Europe. President Harry S. Truman

Hoover traveled to nearly 40 countries in 1946. While in Poland, he visited orphans. Hoover worked to find food for them and other victims of war.

asked Hoover to lead the Famine Emergency Committee. In 1946, Hoover directed the committee. It fed millions of Europeans while they rebuilt their cities and farms.

In 1947 and 1953, Hoover served as chairman for two special government groups. They suggested ways to cut wasteful spending. The federal government took most of their suggestions. These groups later became known as the Hoover Commissions.

Hoover spent the rest of his days writing, giving speeches, and advising American presidents. By 1963, Hoover had grown ill. Yet he refused to give up his work. On October 20, 1964, Herbert Hoover died in New York City. He is buried near his childhood home in West Branch, Iowa.

Though he was known as a great problem solver, Herbert Hoover faced a difficult presidency. Americans blamed him for the Great Depression. But the problems that caused the depression were firmly in place when he

Herbert and Lou Hoover are buried beside each other. Their graves overlook Hoover's birthplace in West Branch, Iowa.

took office. Not even Hoover's leadership skills could overcome them. Yet later in life, Hoover regained America's respect and praise for his hard work.

Hoover's life after his presidency was active. In 1960, he still worked 8 to 12 hours per day.

OFFICE OF THE PRESIDENT

BRANCHES OF GOVERNMENT

The U.S. government is divided into three branches. They are the executive, legislative, and judicial branches. This division is called a separation of powers. Each branch has some power over the others. This is called a system of checks and balances.

EXECUTIVE BRANCH

The executive branch enforces laws. It is made up of the president, the vice president, and the president's cabinet. The president represents the United States around the world. He or she oversees relations with other countries and signs treaties. The president signs bills into law and appoints officials and federal judges. He or she also leads the military and manages government workers.

LEGISLATIVE BRANCH

The legislative branch makes laws, maintains the military, and regulates trade. It also has the power to declare war. This branch consists of the Senate and the House of Representatives. Together, these two houses make up Congress. Each state has two senators. A state's population determines the number of representatives it has.

JUDICIAL BRANCH

The judicial branch interprets laws. It consists of district courts, courts of appeals, and the Supreme Court. District courts try cases. If a person disagrees with a trial's outcome, he or she may appeal. If the courts of appeals support the ruling, a person may appeal to the Supreme Court. The Supreme Court also makes sure that laws follow the U.S. Constitution.

QUALIFICATIONS FOR OFFICE

To be president, a person must meet three requirements. A candidate must be at least 35 years old and a natural-born U.S. citizen. He or she must also have lived in the United States for at least 14 years.

ELECTORAL COLLEGE

The U.S. presidential election is an indirect election. Voters from each state choose electors to represent them in the Electoral College. The number of electors from each state is based on population. Each elector has one electoral vote. Electors are pledged to cast their vote for the candidate who receives the highest number of popular votes in their state. A candidate must receive the majority of Electoral College votes to win.

TERM OF OFFICE

Each president may be elected to two four-year terms. Sometimes, a president may only be elected once. This happens if he or she served more than two years of the previous president's term.

The presidential election is held on the Tuesday after the first Monday in November. The president is sworn in on January 20 of the following year. At that time, he or she takes the oath of office:

I do solemnly swear (or affirm) that I will faithfully execute the office of President of the United States, and will to the best of my ability, preserve, protect and defend the Constitution of the United States.

LINE OF SUCCESSION

The Presidential Succession Act of 1947 defines who becomes president if the president cannot serve. The vice president is first in the line of succession. Next are the Speaker of the House and the President Pro Tempore of the Senate. If none of these individuals is able to serve, the office falls to the president's cabinet members. They would take office in the order in which each department was created:

Secretary of State

Secretary of the Treasury

Secretary of Defense

Attorney General

Secretary of the Interior

Secretary of Agriculture

Secretary of Commerce

Secretary of Labor

Secretary of Health and Human Services

Secretary of Housing and Urban Development

Secretary of Transportation

Secretary of Energy

Secretary of Education

Secretary of Veterans Affairs

Secretary of Homeland Security

Benefits

• While in office, the president receives a salary of $400,000 each year. He or she lives in the White House and has 24-hour Secret Service protection.

• The president may travel on a Boeing 747 jet called Air Force One. The airplane can accommodate 70 passengers. It has kitchens, a dining room, sleeping areas, and a conference room. It also has fully equipped offices with the latest communications systems. Air Force One can fly halfway around the world before needing to refuel. It can even refuel in flight!

• If the president wishes to travel by car, he or she uses Cadillac One. Cadillac One is a Cadillac Deville. It has been modified with heavy armor and communications systems. The president takes Cadillac One along when visiting other countries if secure transportation will be needed.

• The president also travels on a helicopter called Marine One. Like the presidential car, Marine One accompanies the president when traveling abroad if necessary.

• Sometimes, the president needs to get away and relax with family and friends. Camp David is the official presidential retreat. It is located in the cool, wooded mountains in Maryland. The U.S. Navy maintains the retreat, and the U.S. Marine Corps keeps it secure. The camp offers swimming, tennis, golf, and hiking.

• When the president leaves office, he or she receives Secret Service protection for ten more years. He or she also receives a yearly pension of $191,300 and funding for office space, supplies, and staff.

PRESIDENTS AND THEIR TERMS

PRESIDENT	PARTY	TOOK OFFICE	LEFT OFFICE	TERMS SERVED	VICE PRESIDENT
George Washington	None	April 30, 1789	March 4, 1797	Two	John Adams
John Adams	Federalist	March 4, 1797	March 4, 1801	One	Thomas Jefferson
Thomas Jefferson	Democratic-Republican	March 4, 1801	March 4, 1809	Two	Aaron Burr, George Clinton
James Madison	Democratic-Republican	March 4, 1809	March 4, 1817	Two	George Clinton, Elbridge Gerry
James Monroe	Democratic-Republican	March 4, 1817	March 4, 1825	Two	Daniel D. Tompkins
John Quincy Adams	Democratic-Republican	March 4, 1825	March 4, 1829	One	John C. Calhoun
Andrew Jackson	Democrat	March 4, 1829	March 4, 1837	Two	John C. Calhoun, Martin Van Buren
Martin Van Buren	Democrat	March 4, 1837	March 4, 1841	One	Richard M. Johnson
William H. Harrison	Whig	March 4, 1841	April 4, 1841	Died During First Term	John Tyler
John Tyler	Whig	April 6, 1841	March 4, 1845	Completed Harrison's Term	Office Vacant
James K. Polk	Democrat	March 4, 1845	March 4, 1849	One	George M. Dallas
Zachary Taylor	Whig	March 5, 1849	July 9, 1850	Died During First Term	Millard Fillmore

PRESIDENT	PARTY	TOOK OFFICE	LEFT OFFICE	TERMS SERVED	VICE PRESIDENT
Millard Fillmore	Whig	July 10, 1850	March 4, 1853	Completed Taylor's Term	Office Vacant
Franklin Pierce	Democrat	March 4, 1853	March 4, 1857	One	William R.D. King
James Buchanan	Democrat	March 4, 1857	March 4, 1861	One	John C. Breckinridge
Abraham Lincoln	Republican	March 4, 1861	April 15, 1865	Served One Term, Died During Second Term	Hannibal Hamlin, Andrew Johnson
Andrew Johnson	Democrat	April 15, 1865	March 4, 1869	Completed Lincoln's Second Term	Office Vacant
Ulysses S. Grant	Republican	March 4, 1869	March 4, 1877	Two	Schuyler Colfax, Henry Wilson
Rutherford B. Hayes	Republican	March 3, 1877	March 4, 1881	One	William A. Wheeler
James A. Garfield	Republican	March 4, 1881	September 19, 1881	Died During First Term	Chester Arthur
Chester Arthur	Republican	September 20, 1881	March 4, 1885	Completed Garfield's Term	Office Vacant
Grover Cleveland	Democrat	March 4, 1885	March 4, 1889	One	Thomas A. Hendricks
Benjamin Harrison	Republican	March 4, 1889	March 4, 1893	One	Levi P. Morton
Grover Cleveland	Democrat	March 4, 1893	March 4, 1897	One	Adlai E. Stevenson
William McKinley	Republican	March 4, 1897	September 14, 1901	Served One Term, Died During Second Term	Garret A. Hobart, Theodore Roosevelt

PRESIDENT	PARTY	TOOK OFFICE	LEFT OFFICE	TERMS SERVED	VICE PRESIDENT
Theodore Roosevelt	Republican	September 14, 1901	March 4, 1909	Completed McKinley's Second Term, Served One Term	Office Vacant, Charles Fairbanks
William Taft	Republican	March 4, 1909	March 4, 1913	One	James S. Sherman
Woodrow Wilson	Democrat	March 4, 1913	March 4, 1921	Two	Thomas R. Marshall
Warren G. Harding	Republican	March 4, 1921	August 2, 1923	Died During First Term	Calvin Coolidge
Calvin Coolidge	Republican	August 3, 1923	March 4, 1929	Completed Harding's Term, Served One Term	Office Vacant, Charles Dawes
Herbert Hoover	Republican	March 4, 1929	March 4, 1933	One	Charles Curtis
Franklin D. Roosevelt	Democrat	March 4, 1933	April 12, 1945	Served Three Terms, Died During Fourth Term	John Nance Garner, Henry A. Wallace, Harry S. Truman
Harry S. Truman	Democrat	April 12, 1945	January 20, 1953	Completed Roosevelt's Fourth Term, Served One Term	Office Vacant, Alben Barkley
Dwight D. Eisenhower	Republican	January 20, 1953	January 20, 1961	Two	Richard Nixon
John F. Kennedy	Democrat	January 20, 1961	November 22, 1963	Died During First Term	Lyndon B. Johnson
Lyndon B. Johnson	Democrat	November 22, 1963	January 20, 1969	Completed Kennedy's Term, Served One Term	Office Vacant, Hubert H. Humphrey
Richard Nixon	Republican	January 20, 1969	August 9, 1974	Completed First Term, Resigned During Second Term	Spiro T. Agnew, Gerald Ford

PRESIDENT	PARTY	TOOK OFFICE	LEFT OFFICE	TERMS SERVED	VICE PRESIDENT
Gerald Ford	Republican	August 9, 1974	January 20, 1977	Completed Nixon's Second Term	Nelson A. Rockefeller
Jimmy Carter	Democrat	January 20, 1977	January 20, 1981	One	Walter Mondale
Ronald Reagan	Republican	January 20, 1981	January 20, 1989	Two	George H.W. Bush
George H.W. Bush	Republican	January 20, 1989	January 20, 1993	One	Dan Quayle
Bill Clinton	Democrat	January 20, 1993	January 20, 2001	Two	Al Gore
George W. Bush	Republican	January 20, 2001	January 20, 2009	Two	Dick Cheney
Barack Obama	Democrat	January 20, 2009			Joe Biden

"The imperative need of this nation at all times is the leadership of Uncommon Men or Women." Herbert Hoover

WRITE TO THE PRESIDENT

You may write to the president at:

**The White House
1600 Pennsylvania Avenue NW
Washington, DC 20500**

You may e-mail the president at:

comments@whitehouse.gov

GLOSSARY

administration - a group of people that manages an operation, a department, or an office. An administrator is a person who works as part of an administration.

blockade - when an army prevents supplies or troops from going into or out of an area.

Boxer Rebellion - in 1900, an uprising in which Chinese peasants tried to force all foreigners from China.

debt - something owed to someone, usually money.

Democrat - a member of the Democratic political party. Democrats believe in social change and strong government.

economy - the way a nation uses its money, goods, and natural resources.

engineer - a person who is skilled in one of the branches of engineering. Engineering is the science or profession of putting matter and energy to use for man.

public works - projects the government pays for, such as roads, dams, or sewers.

Quaker - a member of the religious group called the Society of Friends.

real estate - property, which includes buildings and land.

recession - a time when business activity slows.

Republican - a member of the Republican political party. Republicans are conservative and believe in small government.

running mate - a candidate running for a lower-rank position on an election ticket, especially the candidate for vice president.

seamstress - a woman who sews clothes.

secretary of commerce - a member of the president's cabinet who is in charge of the Department of Commerce. This department manages the nation's economic development.

Speaker of the House - the highest-ranking member of the party with the majority in Congress.

stock market - a place where stocks and bonds, which represent parts of businesses, are bought and sold. Stocks are money that represent part of a business. People who purchase stocks can own part of the company.

treasurer - a person who handles the money for a business, an organization, or a government.

World War I - from 1914 to 1918, fought in Europe. Great Britain, France, Russia, the United States, and their allies were on one side. Germany, Austria-Hungary, and their allies were on the other side.

World War II - from 1939 to 1945, fought in Europe, Asia, and Africa. Great Britain, France, the United States, the Soviet Union, and their allies were on one side. Germany, Italy, Japan, and their allies were on the other side.

WEB SITES

To learn more about Herbert Hoover, visit ABDO Publishing Company on the World Wide Web at **www.abdopublishing.com**. Web sites about Herbert Hoover are featured on our Book Links page. These links are routinely monitored and updated to provide the most current information available.

INDEX